MOVERS,
SHAKERS,
& HISTORY
MAKERS

LIZZO
AWARD-WINNING MUSICIAN

BY KAREN LATCHANA KENNEY

CAPSTONE PRESS
a capstone imprint

Capstone Captivate is published by Capstone Press, an imprint of Capstone.
1710 Roe Crest Drive
North Mankato, Minnesota 56003
www.capstonepub.com

Library of Congress Cataloging-in-Publication Data is available on the Library of Congress website.
Names: Kenney, Karen Latchana, author.
Title: Lizzo : award-winning musician / by Karen Latchana Kenney.
Description: North Mankato, Minnesota : Capstone Press, 2021. |
Series: Movers, shakers, and history makers | Includes bibliographical references and index. Audience: Ages 8-11 | Audience: Grades 4-6 |
Summary: "In September 2019, "Truth Hurts" became the longest-reigning solo female rap song at the number 1 spot on Billboard's Hot 100. Since then, Lizzo has appeared on TV, at award shows, and on sold-out world tours. Learn more about this Grammy-winning artist and how she went from band kid to opening act to mainstream superstar"
Identifiers: LCCN 2020038017 (print) | LCCN 2020038018 (ebook) |
ISBN 9781496695819 (hardcover) | ISBN 9781496697158 (paperback) |
ISBN 9781977154576 (ebook pdf) | ISBN 9781977156242 (kindle edition)
Subjects: LCSH: Lizzo, 1988—Juvenile literature. | Singers—United States—Biography—Juvenile literature. | Rap musicians—United States—Biography—Juvenile literature.
Classification: LCC ML3930.L579 K46 2021 (print) | LCC ML3930.L579 (ebook) |
DDC 782.42164092 [B]—dc23
LC record available at https://lccn.loc.gov/2020038017
LC ebook record available at https://lccn.loc.gov/2020038018

Image Credits
Alamy: TCD/Prod.DB, 40; Associated Press: Sipa USA/Daniel DeSlover, cover (front); Getty Images: Coachella/Frazer Harrison, 38, FilmMagic/Bonnaroo Arts and Music Festival, 31, FilmMagic/Jeff Kravitz, 34, FilmMagic/Tim Mosenfelder, 25, MTV/Randy Shropshire, 33 (top), Pandora/Charley Gallay, 37, Redferns/Richard E. Aaron, 6, The Recording Academy/Emma McIntyre, 42; Newscom: Avalon.red/Retna/B2820, 5, Icon Sportswire/Nick Tre. Smith, 10, Reuters/Caitlin Ochs, 41, ZUMA Press/Daniel DeSlover, 22, ZUMA Press/Jana Birchum, 21, ZUMA Press/Kyndell Harkness, 29, ZUMA Press/Maria Laura Antonelli, 26, ZUMA Press/Nancy Kaszerman, 13, ZUMA Press/Renee Jones Schneider, 27; Shutterstock: arvzdix, 17, Ben Houdijk, 1, Jacob Boomsma, 16, lev radin, 19, Nikola Spasenoski, 9, Rashad Ashur, 39, SkillUp, cover (background), VectorManZone, 15, 33 (bottom), VectorShop, 7

Editorial Credits
Editor: Mari Bolte; Designer: Bobbie Nuytten; Media Researcher: Svetlana Zhurkin; Production Specialist: Katy LaVigne

All internet sites appearing in back matter were available and accurate when this book was sent to press.

TABLE OF CONTENTS

Words in **bold** are in the glossary.

CHAPTER ONE

HERE COMES LIZZO

In the summer of 2019, Lizzo looked out into a massive crowd. She was ready to perform at the Glastonbury Festival in Somerset, England. "I love you. You are beautiful. And you can do anything," she told her audience. The crowd repeated the mantra.

Everyone needs to hear that kind of love. Lizzo— singer, songwriter, rapper, and flutist—knows it. "We can save the world if we save ourselves first," she has said. But the Lizzo of today didn't always feel that self-love herself. It was a long journey to get to that kind of confidence and full-on star status. And it all started in Detroit, Michigan.

The artist known as Lizzo was born Melissa Viviane Jefferson on April 27, 1988. She grew up in Detroit. Her church introduced her to **gospel** music. The music was spiritual, and that connection stuck with her. Young Melissa also loved science and writing, and she studied hard in school. She read **manga** comics. She loved *Sailor Moon*. Sailor Saturn was her favorite character.

Lizzo performing at the Glastonbury Festival in 2019

When Melissa was 9 years old, her family moved to Houston, Texas. It was a big change from Detroit. While her parents worked hard building businesses, Melissa discovered the flute. "I remember in the fifth grade, I just wanted to be really good. I was like, 'I want to be really good at the flute. Everybody else is so bad.'"

James Galway, from Belfast, Ireland, is nicknamed "The Man with the Golden Flute."

The flute was Melissa's start to making music. And she wanted to be the best. She started studying music by listening to it. She listened to James Galway, a famous flute player, and figured out the notes to play his songs on her flute. Later she learned how to read the notes on sheet music.

The flute was a difficult instrument to learn, but Melissa practiced, developed her own style, and excelled. Band was everything to her. Melissa became a proud "band geek."

WHERE HAS LIZZO LIVED?

MINNEAPOLIS, MINNESOTA
MUSIC SCENE

DETROIT, MICHIGAN
BORN

MINNESOTA

MICHIGAN

COLORADO

CALIFORNIA

LOS ANGELES, CALIFORNIA
RECORDING ALBUMS

TEXAS

AURORA, COLORADO
MOM'S HOUSE

HOUSTON, TEXAS
SCHOOL AND FLUTE

HIP-HOP AND DANCE

In her early teens, Melissa discovered hip-hop and dancing. She loved the sounds coming from Destiny's Child and Missy Elliott. She also listened to anime music. "It was so righteous," she said. "Tons of synth, tons of like weird melody and major chords." She realized she wanted to sing and make her own music too.

Every morning before school, Melissa did her own musical ritual in her room. Panic! At the Disco was one of her go-to bands. She blasted music through her speakers and did her own **choreographed** dances. She jumped on her bed and twirled. Even back then, she was a natural performer.

Missy Elliott has won four Grammy awards and is one of the best-selling female rappers in history.

Eighth grade was huge for Melissa. That's when she started calling herself Lizzo. And it's when she formed her first rap crew with two friends from school. They were called the Cornrow Clique.

FACT

Melissa's friends first called her Lizza. Jay-Z's song "Izzo" was popular at the time, so she combined them into Lizzo.

The piccolo is a smaller flute that can play higher notes.

Kids would **freestyle** rap on the bus and in the cafeteria at Lizzo's school. Lizzo learned how to freestyle too. She called into a local morning radio show to freestyle on air. Lizzo loved rapping on the spot, knowing that thousands of people were listening. At age 14, she learned how to twerk. It became one of her best dance moves.

She also joined the marching band that year as a piccolo player. It didn't quite fit the hip-hop image, but Lizzo loved it. "I was the baddest piccolo player in the land, 'cause I got big lungs," she said. But the marching band wasn't exactly popular at her school, and Lizzo was teased for her band-geek persona.

That fit Lizzo just fine. She liked so many different things and didn't quite fit into any one group. But inside, she struggled with how she felt about herself. She wasn't a skinny girl, which seemed to be the ideal. Lizzo hadn't learned how to love herself yet.

CHAPTER TWO

FINDING HER SOUND

Flute continued to be a big part of Lizzo's life. And she was really good. In high school, she took private lessons with the principal flutist for the Houston Ballet Orchestra. Her teacher thought Lizzo was good enough to make it a career. Lizzo had dreams of playing flute in a **symphony** one day. "I really loved . . . sitting in an ensemble and playing music, and I would get goosebumps when we would play pieces," she said.

After high school, Lizzo was awarded a music **scholarship** to attend the University of Houston. She majored in classical flute performance. She hoped to attend the Paris Conservatory in France after she graduated to become even better. In college, Lizzo joined the Cougar Marching Band, playing the piccolo. She was on her way to achieving her symphony dreams.

Lizzo playing flute on the *Today* show in Rockefeller
Plaza in New York in 2019

Despite her enthusiasm for the music program, Lizzo struggled as a musician for the first time during college. She was used to being the best in middle school and high school. She was first chair, or lead, flute in band and always got the solos. Everyone knew who she was, and they knew she was talented. In college, Lizzo had to start over. No one knew her. No one knew what she could do. It was humbling and hard to deal with.

Lizzo left college before her junior year. It didn't seem right for her anymore. She was being pulled more and more into the rap scene and was up late going to shows. Plus, her dad was sick, and there wasn't much money to pay **tuition**. Her mom moved away for a job to help support the family. Lizzo wasn't sure what to do with her life.

"FIRST DAY OUT"
by Tee Grizzley

"WAX SIMULACRA"
by The Mars Volta

**"THEME FROM
JURASSIC PARK"**
by John Williams

"GOODIES"
by Ciara

♫

**LIZZO'S PLAYLIST
OF HER LIFE**

"KNUCK IF YOU BUCK"
by Crime Mob

"THE RAIN"
by Missy Elliott

"WARM WINDS"
by SZA

"LOSE MY BREATH"
by Destiny's Child

15

QUIET DAYS

Lizzo moved in with her mom in Aurora, Colorado, for a summer. She was depressed. She quit playing the flute and making music. But she decided she wanted to try singing. In the evenings, she walked outside and listened to Beyoncé's album *B'Day* and sang along. At first, she wasn't great. But with practice, she got better and better. She decided that was what she wanted to do. Lizzo moved back to Houston to be a singer.

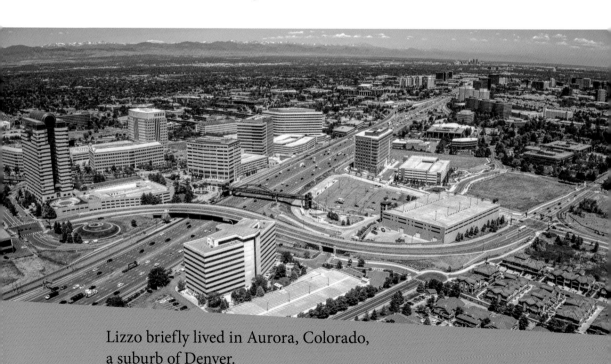

Lizzo briefly lived in Aurora, Colorado, a suburb of Denver.

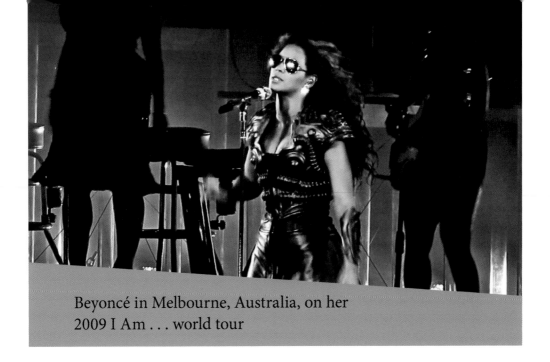

Beyoncé in Melbourne, Australia, on her
2009 I Am . . . world tour

Lizzo started finding her confidence. She decided
she wanted to be a front woman. She auditioned for
a rock band she found on Craigslist. She was nervous
and just went wild in the audition.

The band didn't know what to make of her
but decided she was good and let her in. Their
first performance together helped Lizzo learn to
express herself. She screamed a lot in the band and
experimented with her voice. It was good training.
She was becoming a stronger singer and performer.

FACT

The band Lizzo joined was Ellypseas. One newspaper
called the band's sound "a particular brand of strange."

In 2009, Lizzo's whole world fell apart when her dad died. He had always been her biggest musical supporter. On top of that, the band wasn't doing well.

Money was tight—some nights the singer went to bed without a meal. Hungry and homeless, Lizzo slept in the band's practice space, on friends' couches and floors, and later in her car. She fell into a deep depression again.

Lizzo was feeling lost. Then she started going to therapy. It helped her remember who she was.

There was one more thing that was bothering her. Lizzo had struggled with her body image for much of her life. She'd always thought she had to lose weight, change her hair, or have lighter-colored skin to be accepted as a person and a musician.

One day, she woke up and decided to make a change. She thought, "This is it. Twenty-some-odd years of me believing that one day I'd wake up and be some other girl. You're going to look this way for the rest of your life. And you have to be OK with that." And that's what Lizzo did.

Lizzo at *Bustle*'s 2019 Rule Breakers Festival, which celebrates those who "refuse to do what they're told"

CHAPTER THREE

INDIE GROUPS TO SHININ' SOLO

In 2010, her band Ellypseas broke up. Lizzo wasn't sure what to do. Should she even continue making music? She moved back to Colorado with her mother while she decided.

Lizzo had met electronic musician and producer Johnny Lewis when she lived in Colorado before. He was from Minneapolis, Minnesota. They'd been creating music through Skype and email for a while. Johnny made the beats, and Lizzo sang.

She went to the South by Southwest music festival in Austin, Texas. Many of the bands performing were from Minneapolis. It was clear that something big was happening in music there. Johnny asked Lizzo to move to Minneapolis and start a band.

Lizzo made the move north to Minneapolis in 2011. She didn't really know anyone there or much about the city. But it was a decision that ended up changing her life.

South by Southwest music festival fans watch a performance by Stone Temple Pilots in 2010.

Lizzo and Sophia Eris performed together
in 2016 in Tennessee.

MINNEAPOLIS BANDS

Johnny and Lizzo called their band Lizzo and
the Larva Ink. Their sound was a funky mix of
electronic, pop, soul, and hip-hop music. They started
performing locally, and Lizzo quickly became part

of the music scene. Johnny introduced her to other Minneapolis musicians. Soon Lizzo was singing and rapping with different artists.

She **collaborated** on a mix tape. She also joined several hip-hop groups. Two of the first were Tha Clerb and The Chalice. The Chalice included musicians Sophia Eris and Claire De Lune. Both were also well-known in the Minneapolis music scene. The women sang and rapped, and they quickly had some local hits.

"Push It" by The Chalice was picked up by The Current, a local radio station. A DJ had them on-air for an interview and asked when their album was dropping. They started booking more shows.

In 2012, local paper the *City Pages* named The Chalice the Best New Artist. The next year, Lizzo, DJs Sophia Eris and Shannon Blowtorch, and rapper Manchita formed GRRRL PRTY. This all-female group not only sang and rapped, they danced too. Their sound was described as "a celebration of femininity and unsheathed swagger."

GOING SOLO

Lizzo had always been part of groups, and they were having some success. But she wanted to do her own thing too. So she started working on some solo songs. She met artist and producer Aaron Mader, also called Lazerbeak. He was part of the hip-hop group Doomtree. Along with producer Ryan Olson, they worked on Lizzo's first solo album, *Lizzobangers*. It released in 2013 and had a gritty and tough sound.

The album got some respect locally and around the world. Soon Lizzo was touring the United States, Canada, and the United Kingdom. She opened for Har Mar Superstar, another Twin Cities musician getting attention. From Scotland to San Diego, Lizzo's reputation and her audience were growing.

FACT

Lizzo met Lazerbeak through Twitter. She posted that she wished she could afford to buy one of his beats. Lazerbeak answered.

Lazerbeak in Austin, Texas, in 2015

WRITING LYRICS

Where do Lizzo's catchy lyrics come from? Her conversations. She told the story of coming up with "Batches and Cookies." She was walking down the street with her best friend Sophia and said, "I got my batches and cookies. And that's all I need, girl." That line became a lyric in her first solo song.

PLAYING FOR PRINCE

Another big local and world-famous musician noticed Lizzo's talent. Prince saw The Chalice on a **documentary** about Minnesota music. He knew talent when he saw it. He invited Lizzo and Sophia Eris to Paisley Park, his music studio in Minnesota. He wanted them to rap on the track "BOYTROUBLE" for his group 3RDEYEGIRL.

Being recognized by Prince was a huge honor. Prince was a legend in the music industry. He recorded 39 albums during his career. Sixteen of those had gone **platinum**. Lizzo had only been in Minneapolis for a year. Now she was recording with the world-famous Prince.

At the studio, Prince told Lizzo and Sophia to do whatever they wanted. They did some rapping. Lizzo even screamed. Prince left it all in. Later, Prince asked them to come back to play at parties at Paisley Park. The music **icon** even offered to produce Lizzo's album.

Prince, 2016

Although Prince died before the album could happen, the offer boosted Lizzo's confidence in her talent. It kept her going. It was tough trying to break into the **mainstream** music industry. But she had a good foot in the door.

Lizzo performed for a huge crowd in Minneapolis to honor Prince the day he died, April 21, 2016.

CHAPTER FOUR

FREESTYLE FLOW

Lizzo hit the studio again. She recorded her second solo album, filling it with personal songs. They showed off her range and talent. Released in 2015, *Big GRRRL Small World* got major critics' attention. *Spin* magazine named it one of the 50 best hip-hop albums of 2015.

One of the songs on that album was especially raw and honest. "My Skin" is a **ballad** about learning to love yourself. It describes the black female experience in a country where racism is a real problem. Many people of color in America feel as though their skin is all that is seen—not their behaviors, achievements, or worth.

As a child, Lizzo sometimes wished she could wake up in new skin. But as she came to know herself, she came to love herself. And she knows her lyrics have power. The message of "My Skin" is a love letter to all women with brown skin.

I woke up in this, I woke up in this
In my skin
I can't wash it away, so you can't take it from me
My brown skin.

Lizzo was called "the body-positive rapper" in a *Billboard* online article in 2015.

MAJOR LABEL ATTENTION

In 2016, Lizzo got something all musicians strive for—a major label record deal. She signed with the Nice Life Recording Company, part of Atlantic Records. It was the beginning of her rise to superstar status. By October, her first major label album released. *Coconut Oil* had six songs. She experimented with freestyling instead of writing lyrics. She had to trust herself to let the words flow in the studio.

FACT

Lizzo's flute has its own name—Sasha Flute, after Beyoncé's alter ego, Sasha Fierce. It also has its own Instagram account (@Sashabefluting).

Coconut Oil featured a flute solo. Lizzo had recorded with the flute before, but she had never brought it onstage. Now Sasha Flute would come on tour.

Lizzo performing at the Bonnaroo Arts and Music Festival in Tennessee, 2016

Lizzo's self-love anthem "Good as Hell" was the first track off of *Coconut Oil*. It was featured in the movie *Barbershop: The Next Cut*, and on the movie's soundtrack. It warmed up fans for what was to come.

That year, Lizzo moved to Los Angeles to be closer to the music industry. She was hosting the MTV show *Wonderland*. She co-hosted the VMA Pre-show with DJ Khaled. But mainstream success still seemed to be out of Lizzo's reach.

In 2017, she released her single "Truth Hurts." She knew it was her best song yet. But she wasn't sure if the world would notice. After all that work, she almost gave up. But her producer, family, and friends convinced her to keep going. The song wasn't big then, but it would be soon.

Lizzo toured for her new album in 2017. The next year, she toured with other bands too, opening for Florence + the Machine and HAIM. She also played at one of the biggest music festivals in the United States. At Lollapalooza, Lizzo joined The Weeknd, Jack White, Bruno Mars, Post Malone, and other headliners. She stood out as one of the best.

Lizzo hosting MTV's *Wonderland* show in 2016

LIZZO'S BANDS

2001
Cornrow Clique

2008
Ellypseas

2011
Lizzo and the Larva Ink

2012
Tha Clerb and The Chalice

2013
GRRRL PRTY

2013-PRESENT
Solo

SOUNDTRACKS AND COMMERCIALS

It wasn't just fans who heard Lizzo's music. Her sound was showing up all over TV and in the movies. "Good as Hell" showed up in other movies, including *A Bad Mom's Christmas* and *I Feel Pretty*. Her music has appeared on the shows *Insecure*, *black-ish*, *grown-ish*, and *The Bold Type*.

Lizzo greets her fans at a music festival in San Francisco in 2018.

Weight Watchers used Lizzo's song "Worship" in their advertising campaign. The company was changing its brand to "WellnessWins." They were focusing on exercise and healthy eating as part of living a well life. Lizzo's fans weren't happy though. Many thought a diet company went against her message of body positivity. In a live Instagram video, Lizzo explained how exercise and treating yourself well is something she believes in.

FACT

Body positivity is the belief that all people deserve to love their bodies. They don't need to be their society's ideal weight or look. They are beautiful as they are.

CHAPTER FIVE

"YOU KNOW YOU A STAR"

It turned out that 2019 was Lizzo's year. In April, she dropped her first full-length album with Atlantic. *Cuz I Love You* would be the album to rocket Lizzo into mainstream success. She even collaborated with one of her musical idols on it. The song "Tempo" features Missy Elliott, with an intro inspired by Prince. "Truth Hurts" was also later added as a bonus track.

FACT

Time magazine named Lizzo "Entertainer of the Year" in 2019.

Then Netflix put "Truth Hurts" on the soundtrack for its movie *Someone Great*. That did it. The song eventually rose to the number 1 spot on the *Billboard Hot 100*. The song that almost made Lizzo quit music was now her breakout hit. At last the world knew who Lizzo was, and they loved her. She was officially a superstar.

A fan promotes Lizzo's song "Worship" at a 2018 event in Los Angeles.

WORLD TOURS

Lizzo had been working hard for a decade to get where she was. Now she was world-famous.

In April 2019, she played at the Coachella Music Festival. A huge crowd came to hear her new music. The set was filled with technical issues though. Her music stopped playing. It could have been a disaster. But Lizzo and her dancers performed through it all. The audience even sang along when the music cut out.

Lizzo and her dancers on stage at Coachella in 2019

Lizzo then went on tour for her album. It sold out so quickly that a second tour was added. She played shows across the United States, Europe, Canada, New Zealand, and Australia. After that she went to the Glastonbury Festival in June, and then back to the United States for summer festivals.

LIZZO'S SOLO ALBUMS

- 2013: LIZZOBANGERS
- 2015: BIG GRRRL SMALL WORLD
- 2016: COCONUT OIL
- 2019: CUZ I LOVE YOU

FACT

When the sound failed at Coachella, Lizzo played the melody on her flute. She also sang **a cappella**.

Along with singing, Lizzo began doing some acting. She performed the voice of Lydia in *UglyDolls*. The animated movie musical also featured other big-name musicians, including Nick Jonas, Janelle Monáe, and Pitbull. Next, she acted in the crime drama *Hustlers*, alongside Jennifer Lopez and Cardi B.

Lizzo voiced the *UglyDolls* character Lydia (second from left).

THE BIG GRRRLS

The Big Grrrls, Lizzo's plus-sized backup dancers, joined her on *Saturday Night Live*. Most artists have slim dancers. But Lizzo chose to have curvy dancers. She wants to promote women of all sizes.

In December 2019, Lizzo was the musical guest on *Saturday Night Live.* The host that night was actor and *SNL* alum Eddie Murphy, who hadn't hosted for 35 years. Lizzo sang "Truth Hurts" with a live band. For her second song, she did "Good as Hell." It was just before the holidays, so Lizzo spread some cheer. She told everyone, "Happy holidays, y'all. Be kind to one another—but most importantly, be good to yourself."

Besides appearing on *SNL* in December 2019, Lizzo also performed at a holiday concert in Madison Square Garden.

Lizzo accepts the Best Pop Solo Performance award for "Truth Hurts" during the 2020 Grammys.

Winning a Grammy award is something musicians dream about. Lizzo was nominated for eight Grammy awards in 2019. She broke a record for the most nominations for any one musician. She won two awards for her songs "Truth Hurts" and "Jerome," and one for her album *Cuz I Love You*. She also performed at the awards ceremony.

When Lizzo accepted her first award, her speech was about love and the power of music. She told the musicians in the audience, "You guys create beautiful music. You guys create connectivity. And as I'm speaking to all . . . in this room, we need to continue to reach out . . . and lift each other up."

Lizzo was talking about her journey. There were times that were hard. She almost gave up. But instead, she kept going. She reached out to others. She made connections and music that meant something to herself and to other people. Lizzo's career is just taking off. This star's music and positivity is a self-love poem to the whole world.

TIMELINE

1988: Melissa Viviane Jefferson is born in Detroit, Michigan

1997: Melissa and her family move to Houston, Texas

1998: Melissa starts playing the flute

2001: The Cornrow Clique rap crew forms; Melissa gets her nickname Lizzo

2006: Lizzo attends the University of Houston on a music scholarship

2008: Lizzo fronts the rock band Ellypseas

2011: Lizzo moves to Minneapolis and plays in the band Lizzo and the Larva Ink

2012: Tha Clerb and The Chalice form, with Lizzo in their crews

2013: The Chalice gets local attention

Lizzo's first solo album, *Lizzobangers,* is released

2014: Lizzo and Sophia Eris rap on Prince's song "BOYTROUBLE"

2015: *Big GRRRL Small World* releases

2016: Lizzo signs with Atlantic Records; she releases *Coconut Oil*

Los Angeles becomes Lizzo's new home

2019: *Cuz I Love You* releases

Netflix releases *Someone Great,* which features "Truth Hurts"

Lizzo is the musical guest on *Saturday Night Live*

2020: Lizzo wins three Grammy awards

GLOSSARY

**a cappella
(AH kuh-PELL-uh)**
singing without instrumental
accompaniment

ballad (BAL-uhd)
a romantic song, often slow

**choreography
(kor-ee-OG-ruh-fee)**
the arrangement of steps,
movements, and required
elements that make up a
routine

**collaborate
(kuh-LAB-uh-rayt)**
to work together

**documentary
(dahk-yuh-MEN-tuh-ree)**
a movie or TV program about
real situations and people

freestyle (FREE-sty-uhl)
a style of improvisation where
lyrics are made up on the spot

gospel (GOSS-puhl)
a religious style of music and
singing

icon (EYE-kon)
a popular and well-known
symbol recognized by many
people

mainstream (MAYN-streem)
popular, trending music
that is distributed to a wide
audience

manga (MAHN-gah)
comic books created in Japan
and read worldwide

platinum (PLAT-n-uhm)
an album that sells 1 million
copies

scholarship (SKOL-ur-ship)
a grant or prize that pays for a
student to go to college or to
follow a course of study

symphony (SIM-fuh-nee)
a large classical orchestra,
including string, wind, brass,
and percussion instruments

tuition (too-ISH-uhn)
money paid to attend a school

READ MORE

Hudalla, Jamie. *Chance the Rapper: Independent Master of Hip-Hop Flow*. North Mankato, MN: Capstone Press, 2021.

London, Martha. *Lizzo*. Lake Elmo, MN: Focus Readers, 2020.

Wilson, Lakita. *Lizzo: Breakout Artist*. Minneapolis: Lerner Publications, 2020.

INTERNET SITES

Grammy Awards: Lizzo
grammy.com/grammys/artists/lizzo

Great Big Story: How Lizzo Found Her Voice
greatbigstory.com/stories/how-lizzo-found-her-voice

National Association for Music Education: Black History Month
nafme.org/my-classroom/black-history-month/notable-african-american-musicians/

INDEX